Eden Mills, Eramosa, Everton, and Hillsburgh Ontario in Colour Photos, Saving Our History One Photo at a Time

Photography
by Barbara Raué
2014

Series Name:
Cruising Ontario

Book 65: Eden Mills and Area

Cover photo: Eramosa Farmhouse

Series Name: Cruising Ontario
Saving Our History One Photo at a Time

Other Books by Barbara Raue

Coins of Gold

Arrows, Indians and Love

The Life and Times of Barbara
Volume 1: Inventions That Have Enhanced My Life
Volume 2: Entertainment That I Have Enjoyed
Volume 3: East Coast Trips
Volume 4: Olympics Have Always Intrigued Me
Volume 5: Wonders of the World
Volume 6: Caribbean Cruises We Have Enjoyed
Volume 7: Animals
Volume 8: Storms and Other Major Disasters in My Lifetime
Volume 9: Wars, Terrorist Attacks and Major Disasters

The Cromwell Family Book

Eden Mills

Eden Mills was established in 1842 with the construction of the first of three mills and called Kribbs Mill. The mills used water power generated by the Eramosa River, which splits into two branches at the village then flows on to join the Speed River in Guelph, and finally to the Grand, the great Canadian Heritage River. When Adam Argo bought the mill he changed the name to Eden Mills, the name for the post office in 1851 with Mr. Argo as the postmaster. In the early days Eden Mills had a hotel, a flour mill, a wagon maker, blacksmith, general store, shoe store, cooper shop and a daily stage. The first church was of the Congregation Faith. During the nineteenth and early part of the twentieth century Eden Mills grew into an important centre of commerce. In addition to its three mills, it boasted an imposing three-storey general store, a hotel (both still standing), post office, smithy, electric railway station, gas station and coffee shop.

Eramosa

Eramosa is located at the crossroads of Highway 124 and Wellington Road 29 east of Guelph.

Everton

Guelph/Eramosa is a township in Wellington County in mid-western Ontario. It partly encircles the city of Guelph from northeast to south southwest of the city.

Rockwood is the main community in the township. Rockwood is located on Highway 7 between Acton and Guelph. The Eramosa River runs through the centre of the village and the river was the source of power for several mills that were built for the original settlement. Limestone was also extracted from the area. The Rockwood Conservation Area is used for swimming, hiking, canoeing, picnicking and camping.

The township also includes the smaller communities of Ariss, Armstrong Mills, Birge Mills, Blue Springs, Brucedale, Centre Inn, Eden Mills, Eramosa, Everton, Marden, Colbertville, Mosborough, Oakvale, Redwood Hills, and Rockcut.

Hillsburgh

Hillsburgh is located southwest of Orangeville on Wellington Road 24.

Table of Contents

Eden Mills

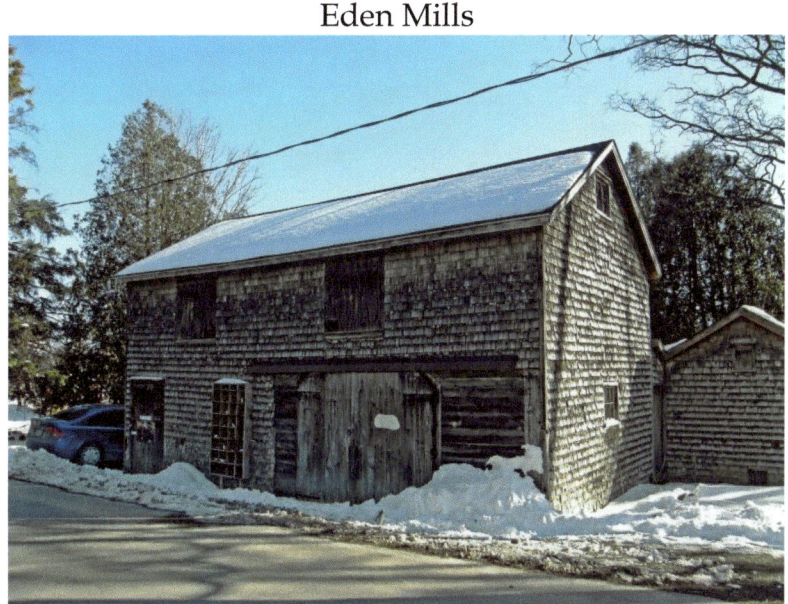

Cedar shake

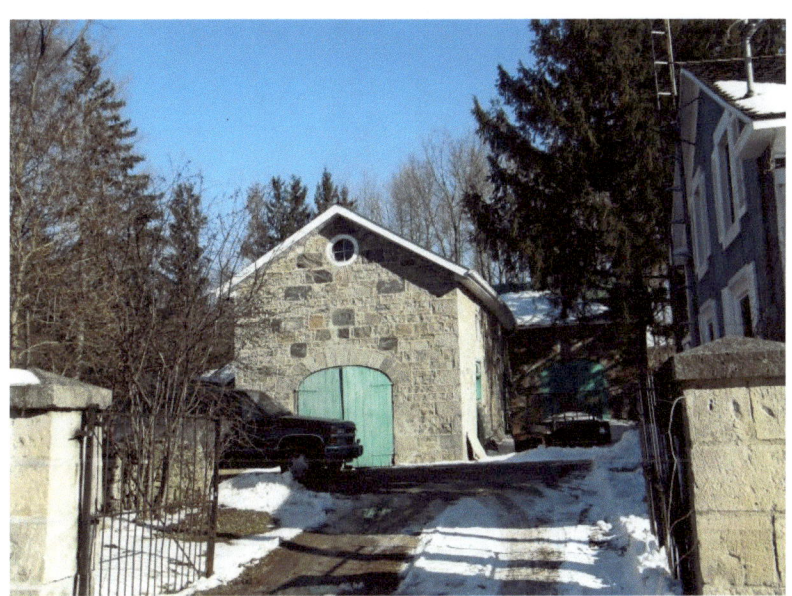

Gothic Revival - cobblestone

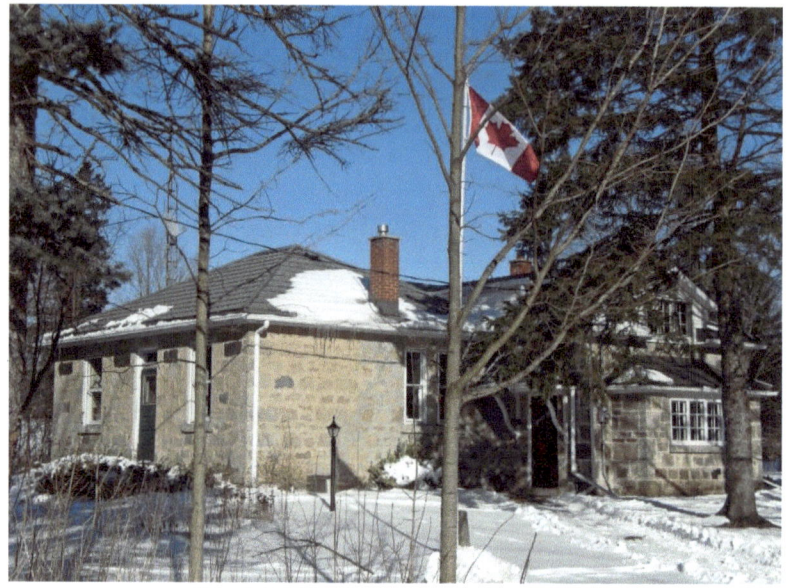

Gothic Revival - cobblestone

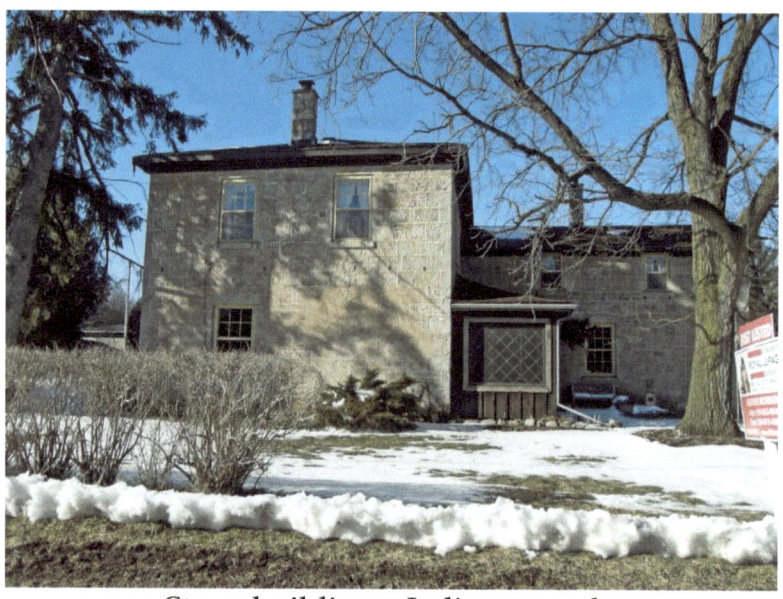

Stone building – Italianate style

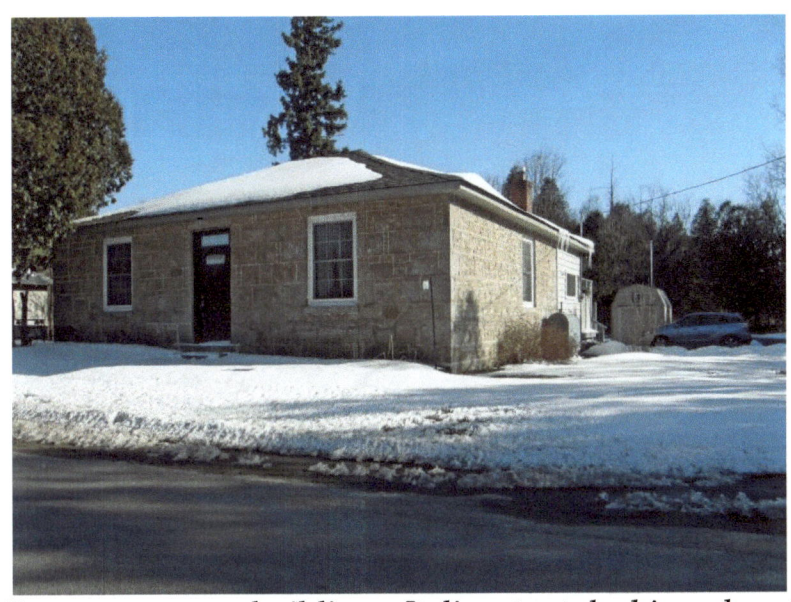

One-storey stone building – Italianate style, hipped roof

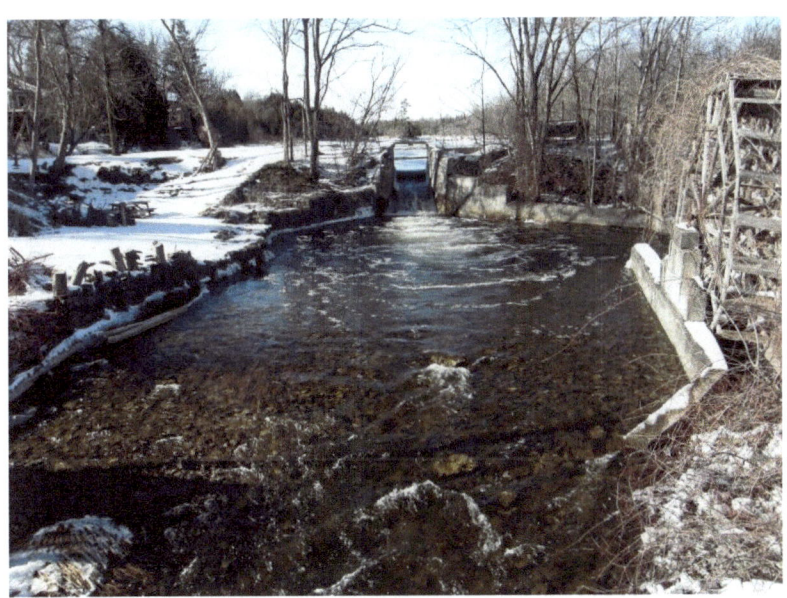

Eramosa River

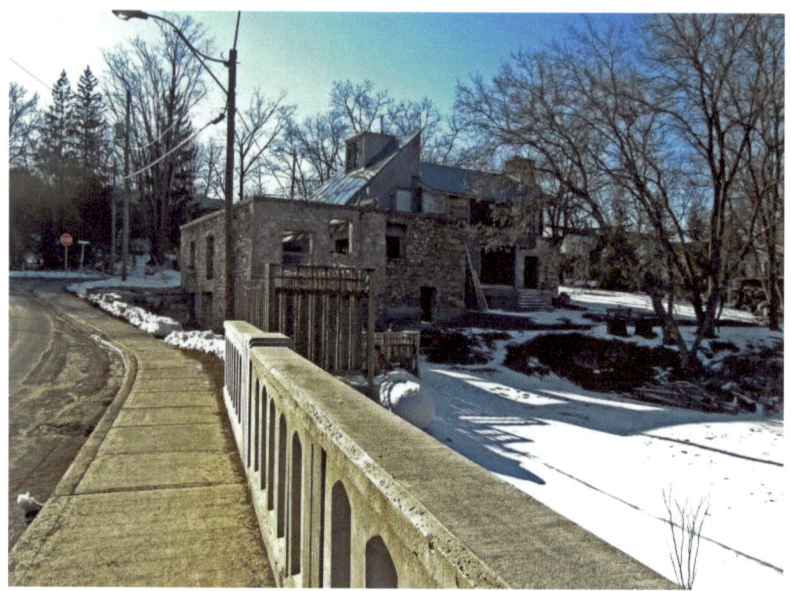

Stone building

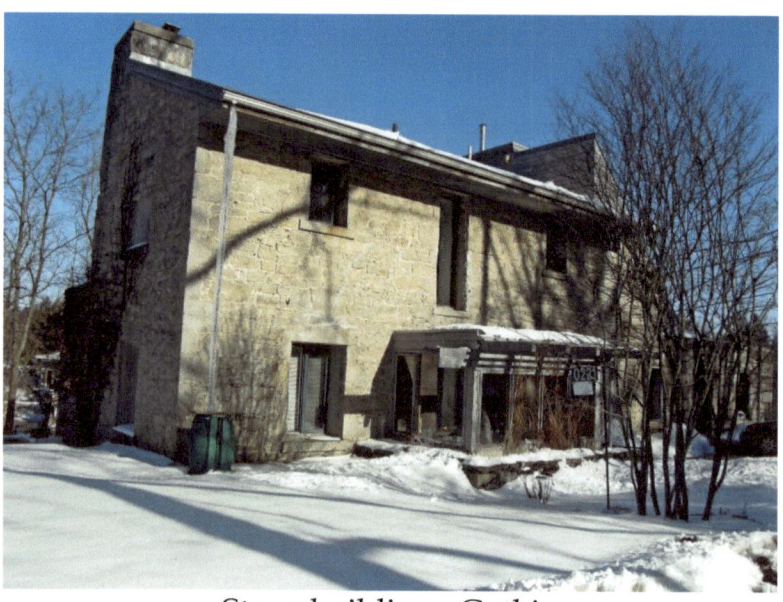

Stone building - Gothic

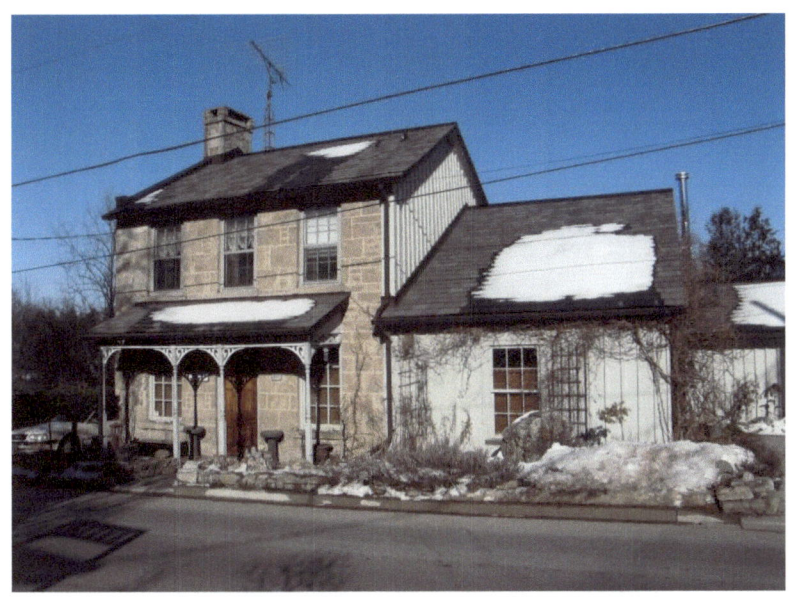

Stone building – Gothic Revival

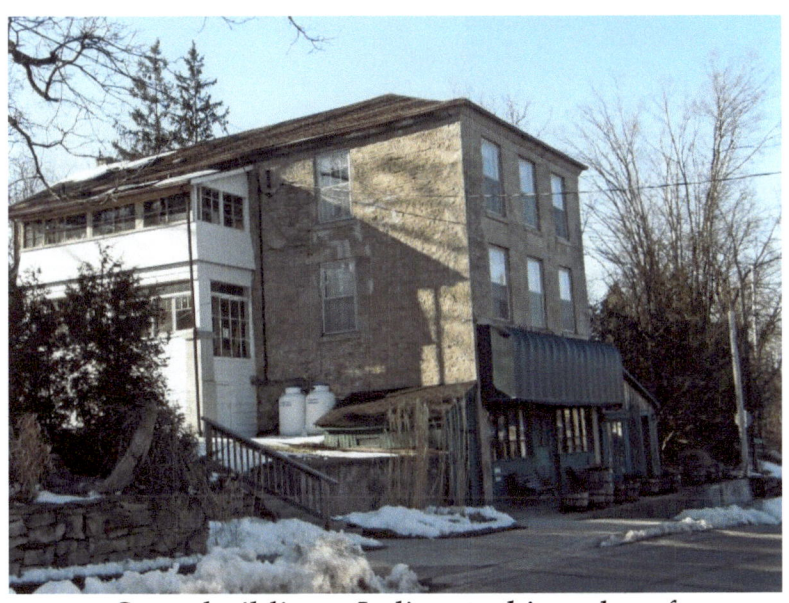

Stone building – Italianate, hipped roof
Three-storey general store

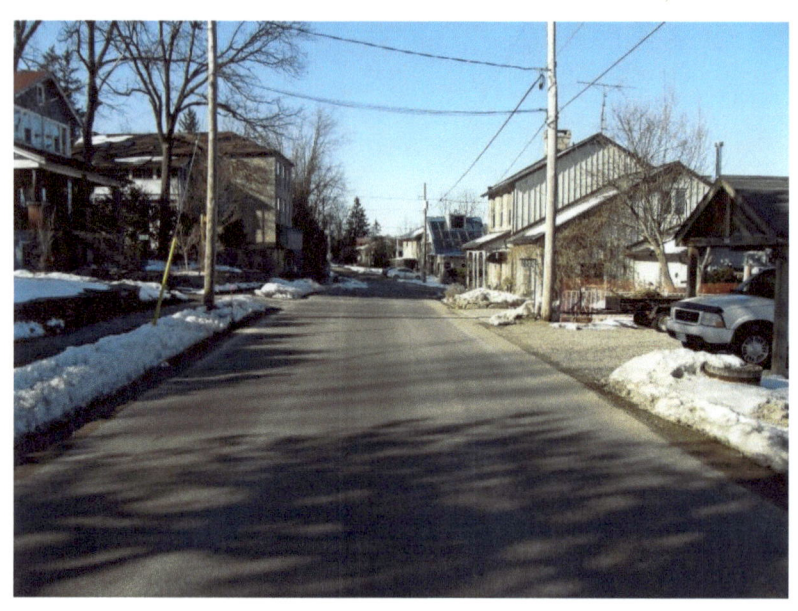

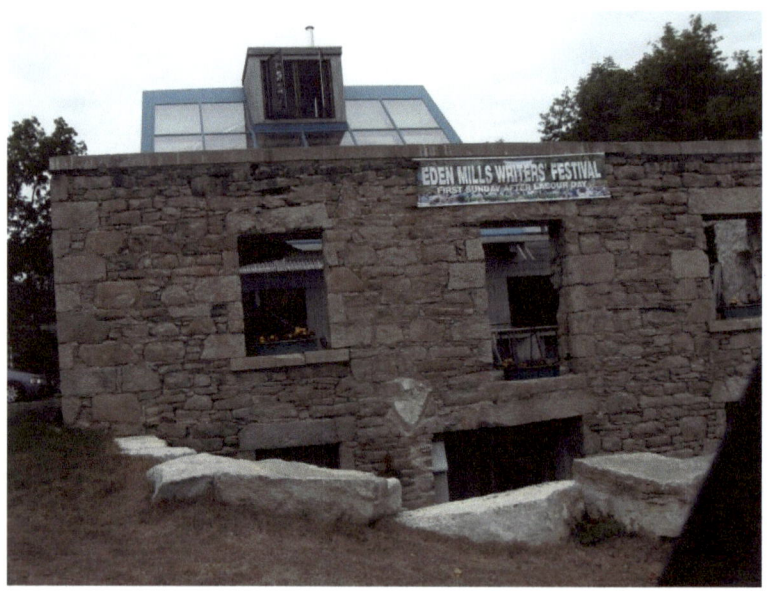

Stone building

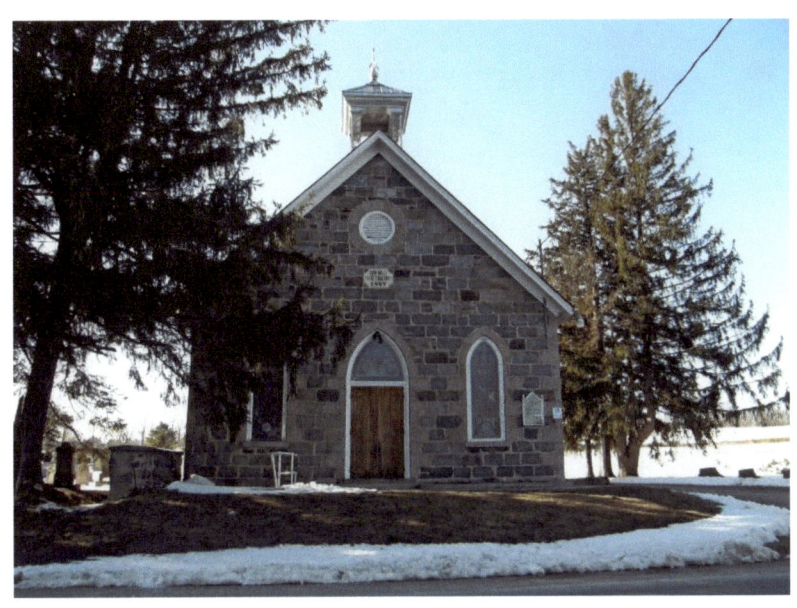

Eden Mills Presbyterian Church – 1887 – Gothic Revival

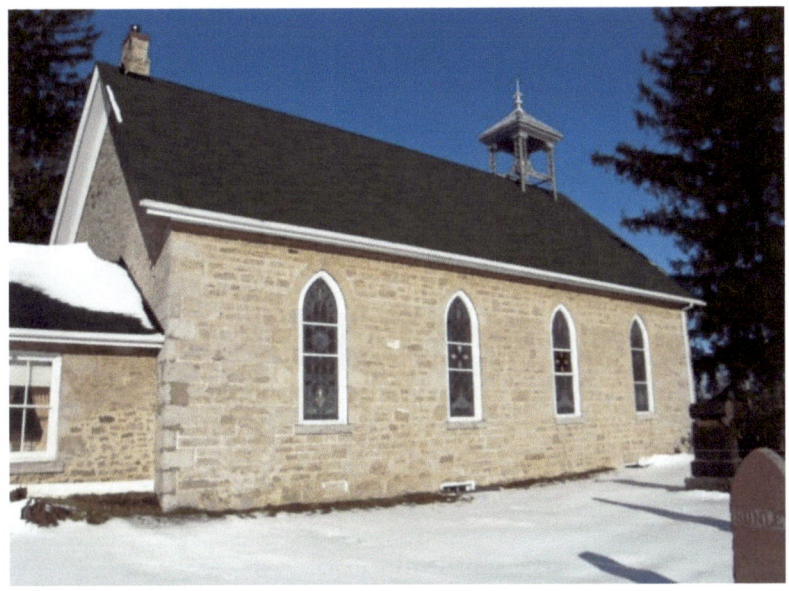

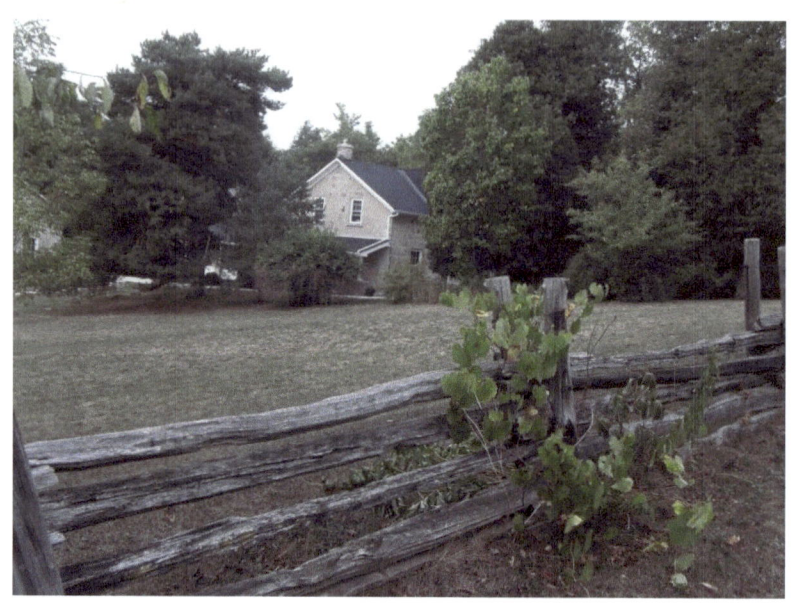

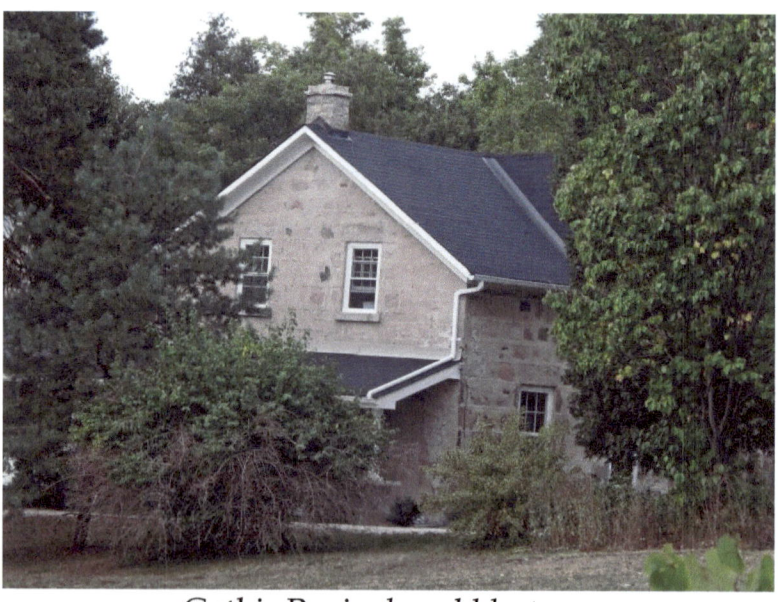

Gothic Revival - cobblestone

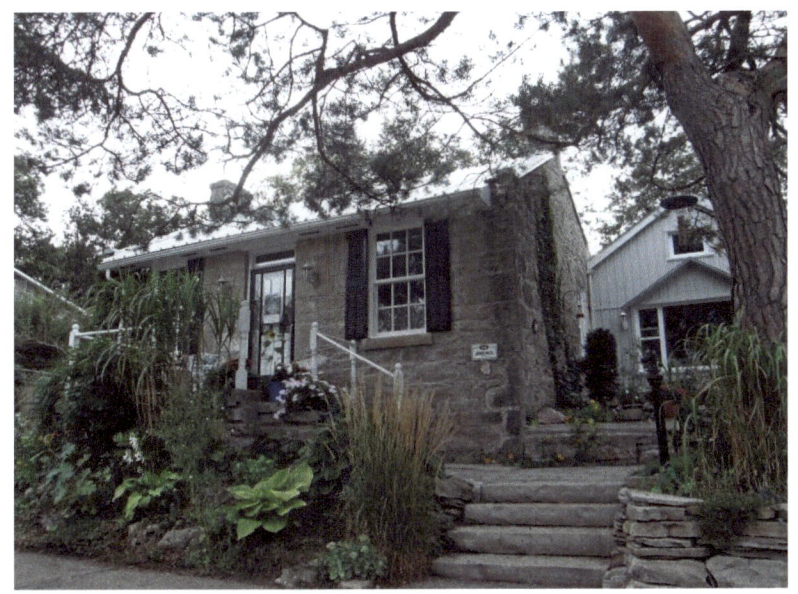

Stone building – Gothic Revival

Eramosa

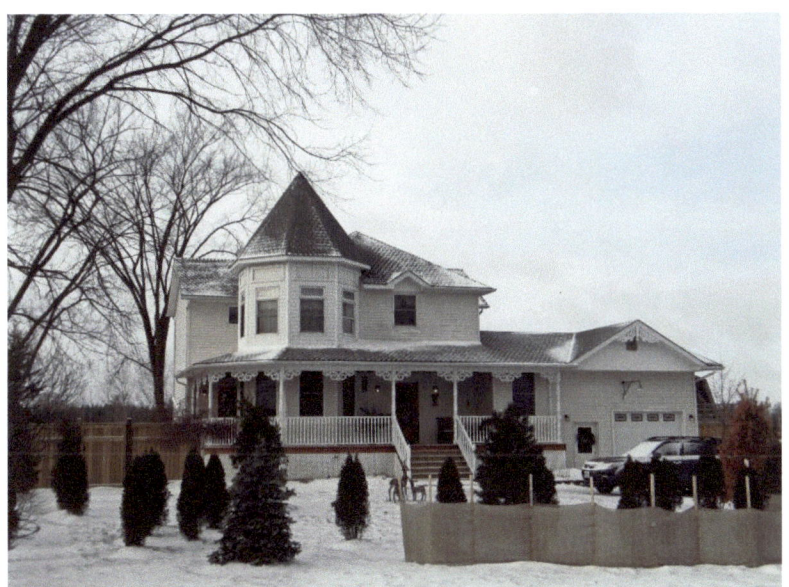

Queen Anne style - turret

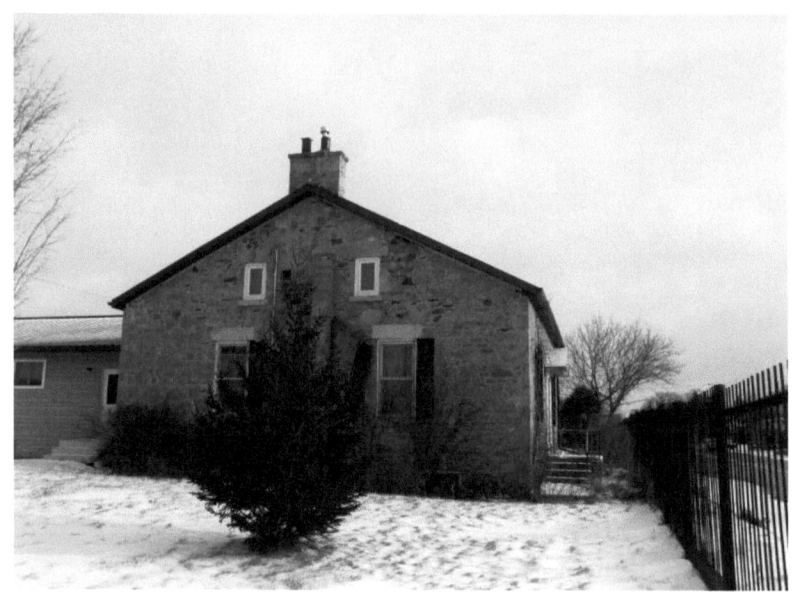

Cobblestone – Gothic Revival

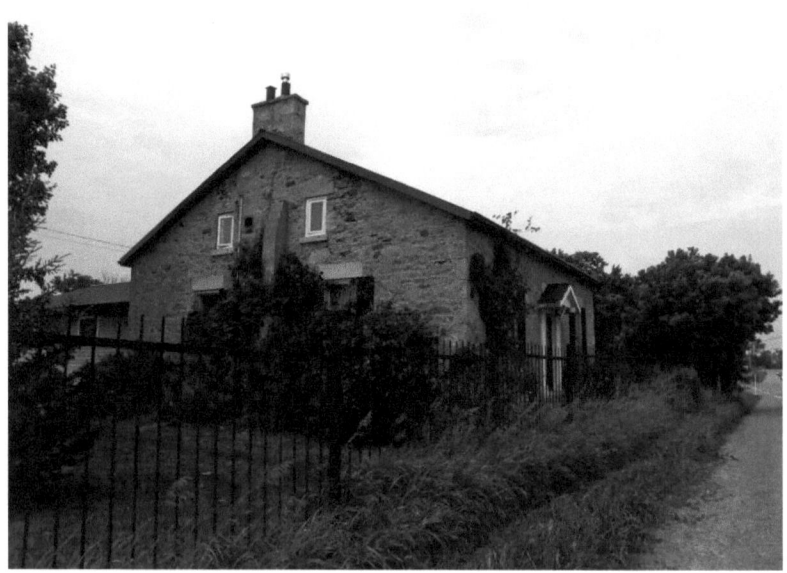

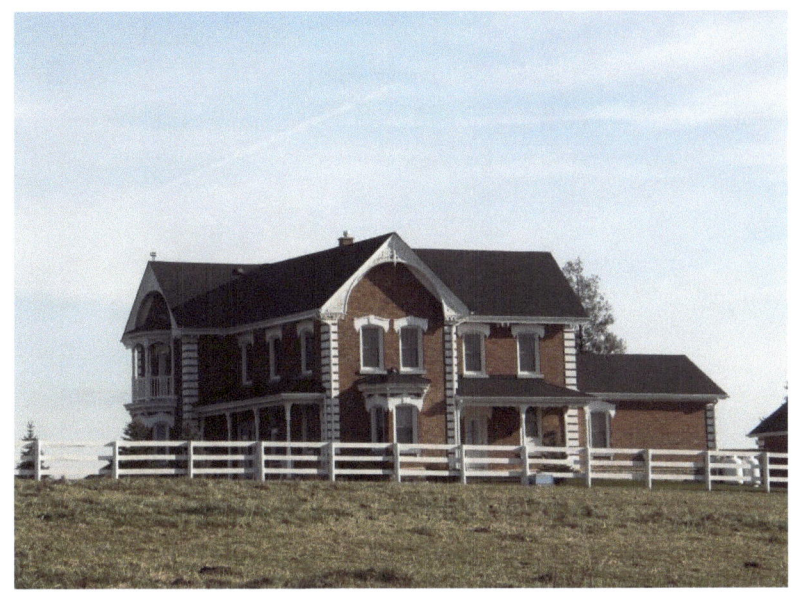

Gothic Revival – corner quoins, bay windows, balconies

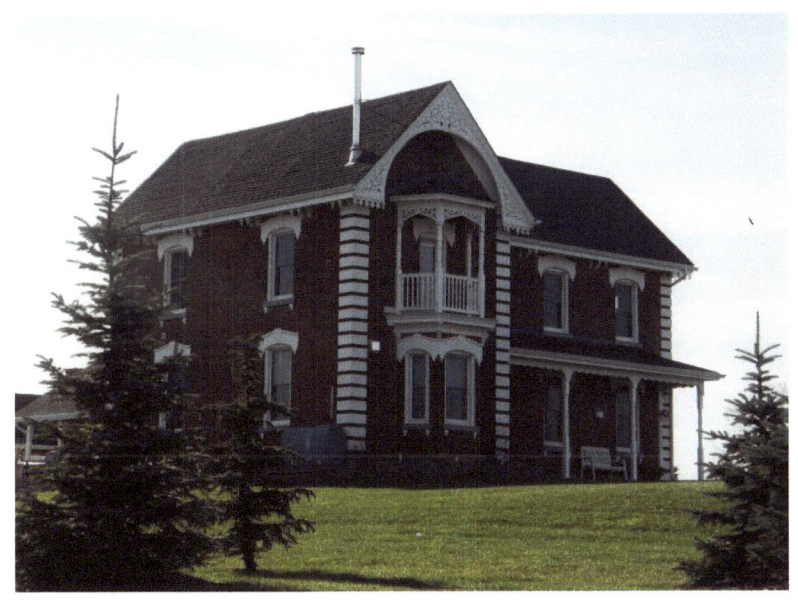

Everton

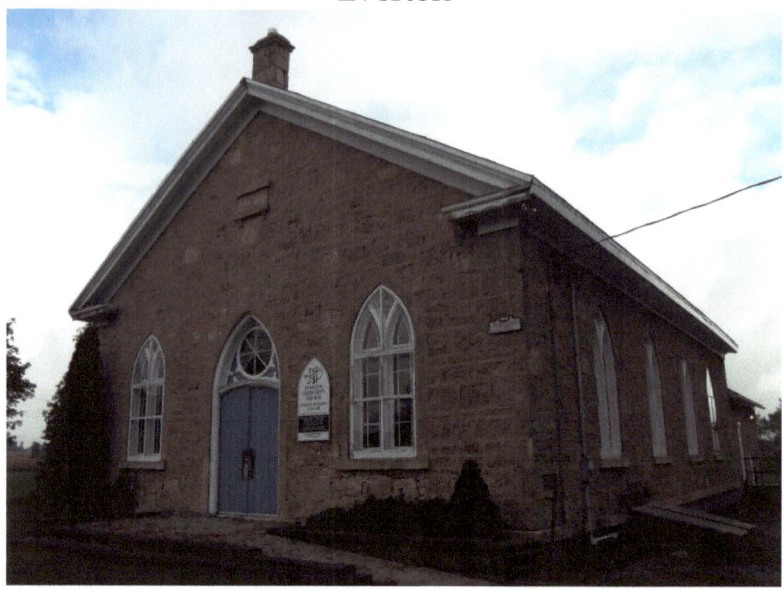

Disciple of Christ 1861
Everton Community Church

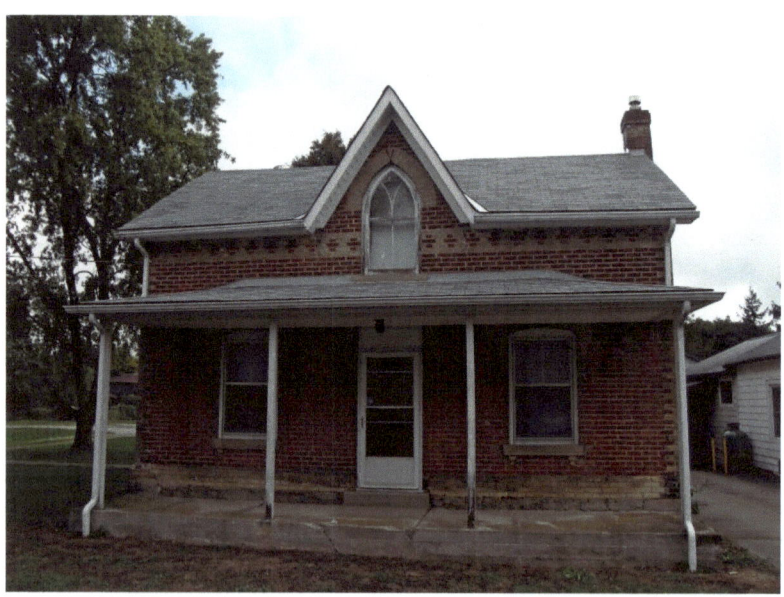

Gothic Revival – dichromatic brickwork

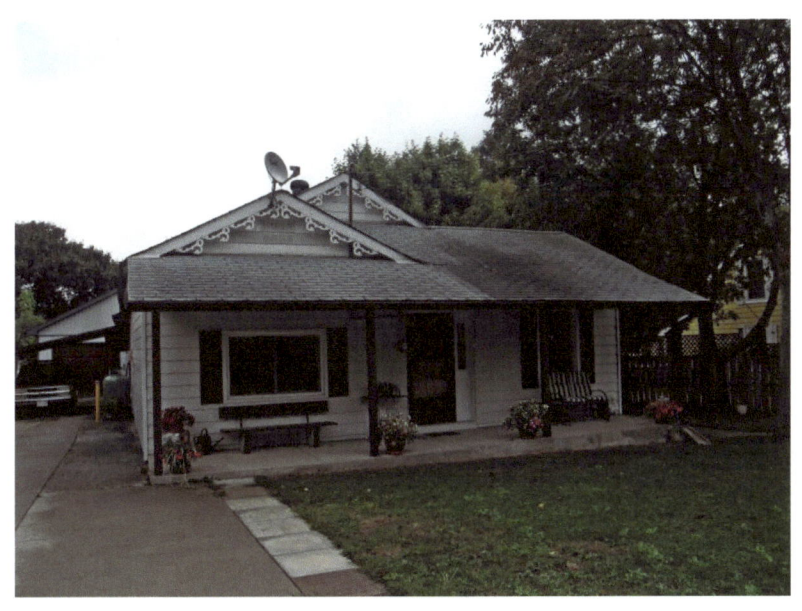

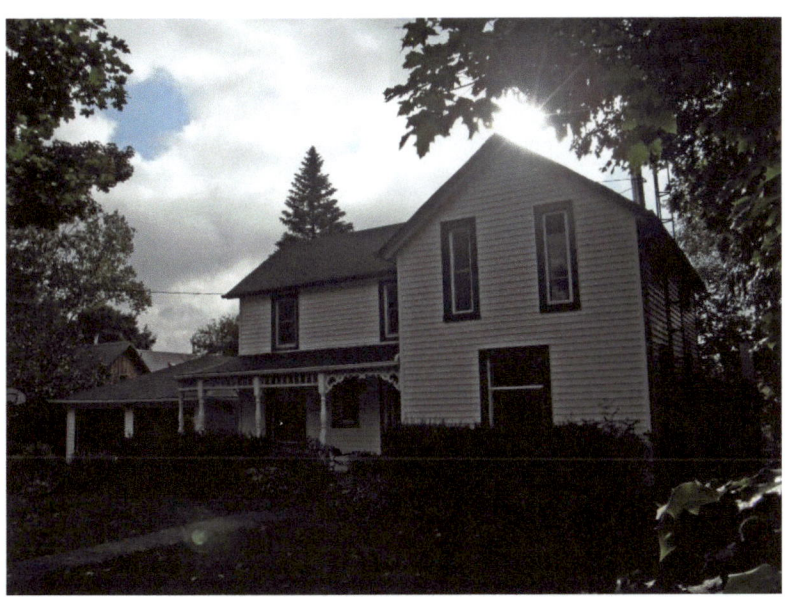

Gothic Revival – E.F. McCullough, Physician - 1880

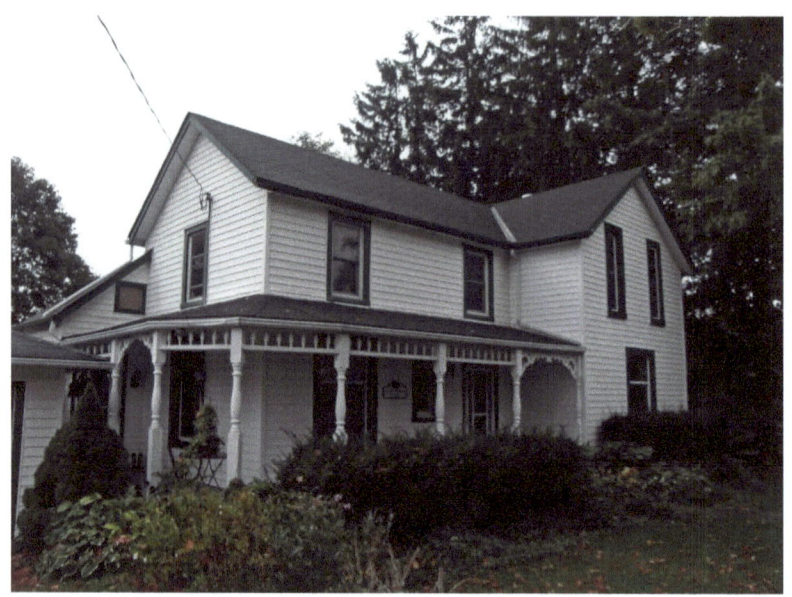

Gothic Revival

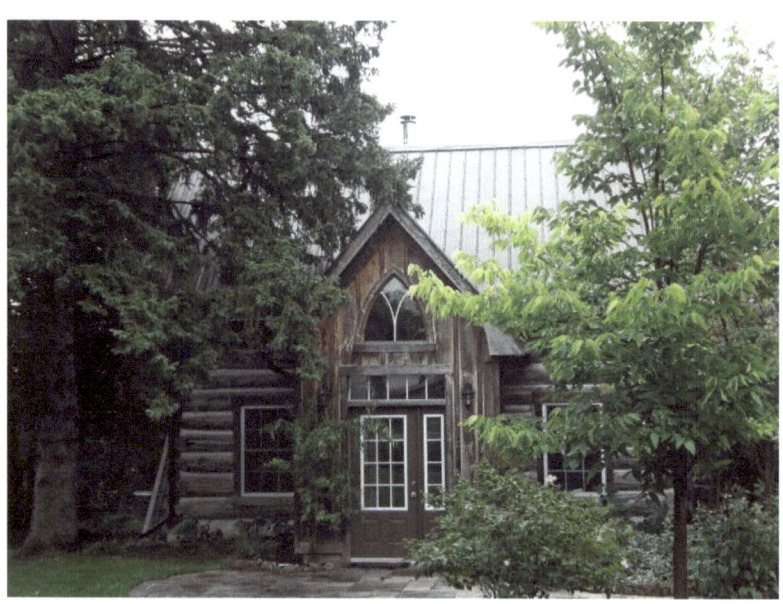

Log Cabin

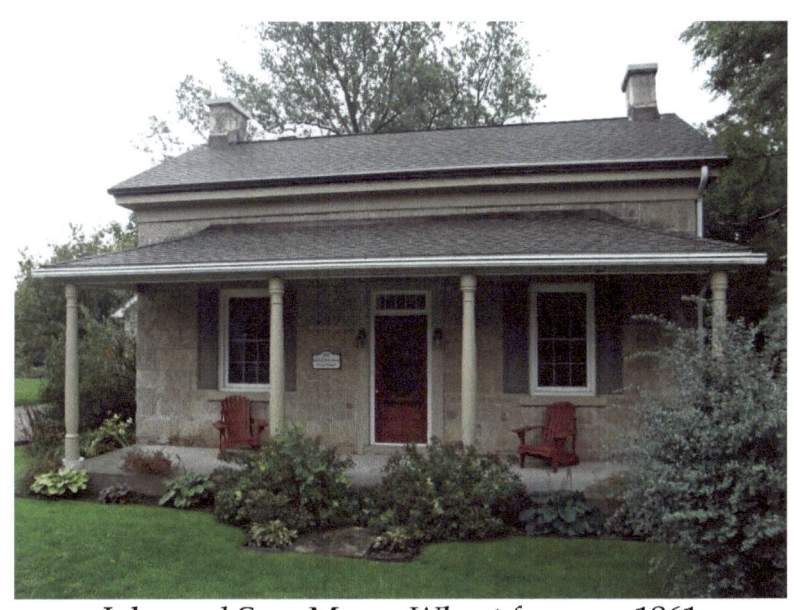

John and Sara Moon, Wheat farmer - 1861

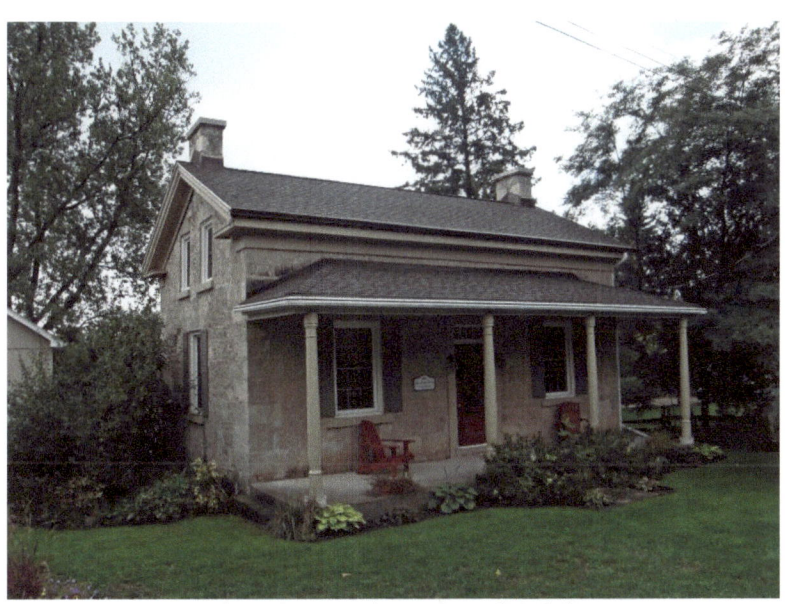

Gothic Revival – stone building

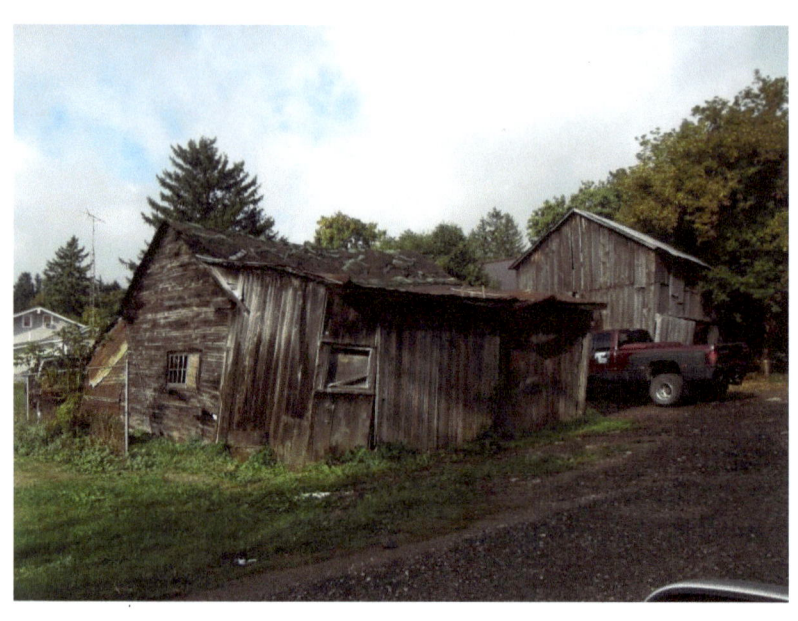

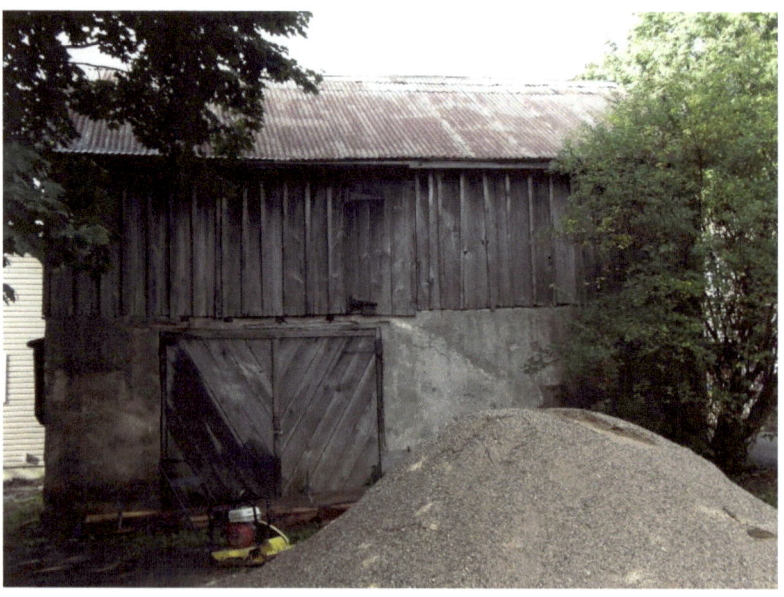

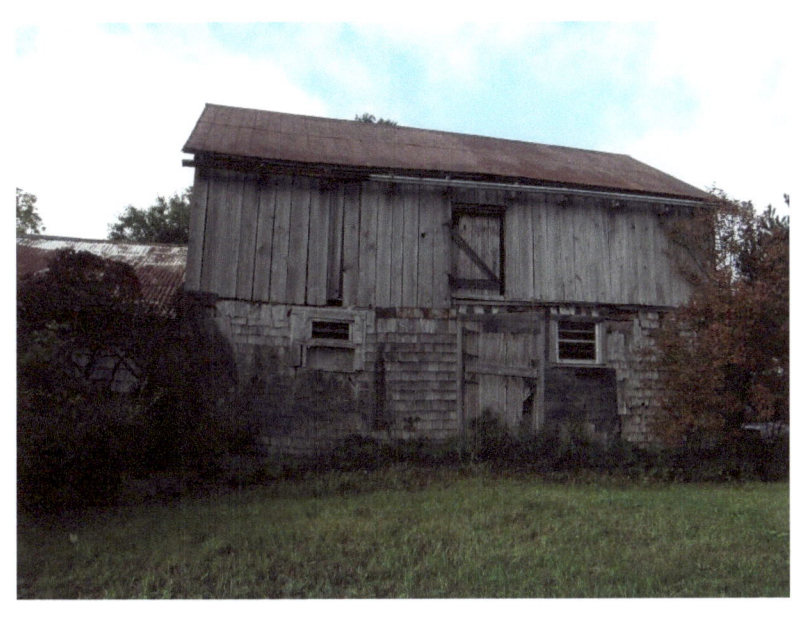

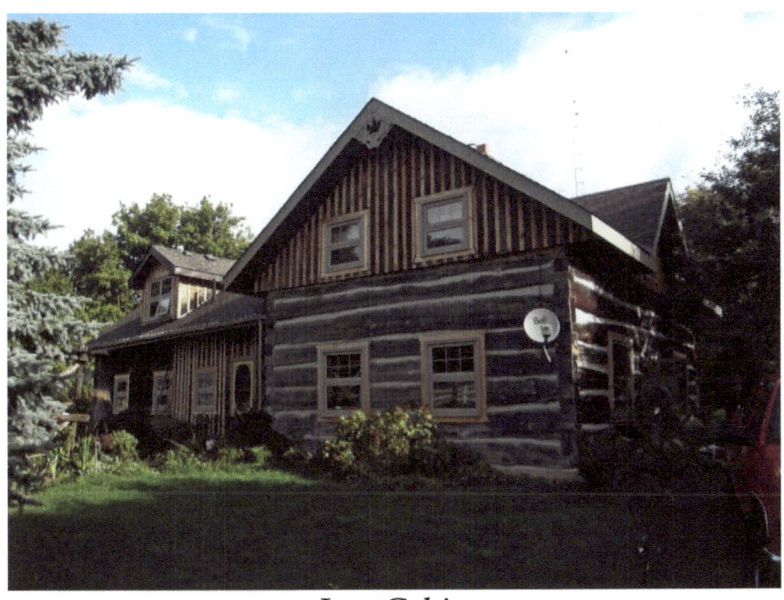

Log Cabin

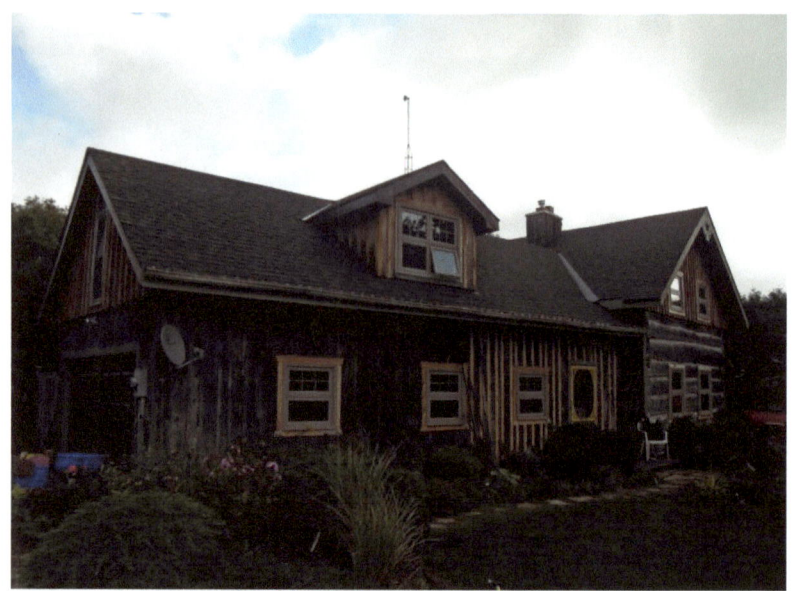

Log Cabin

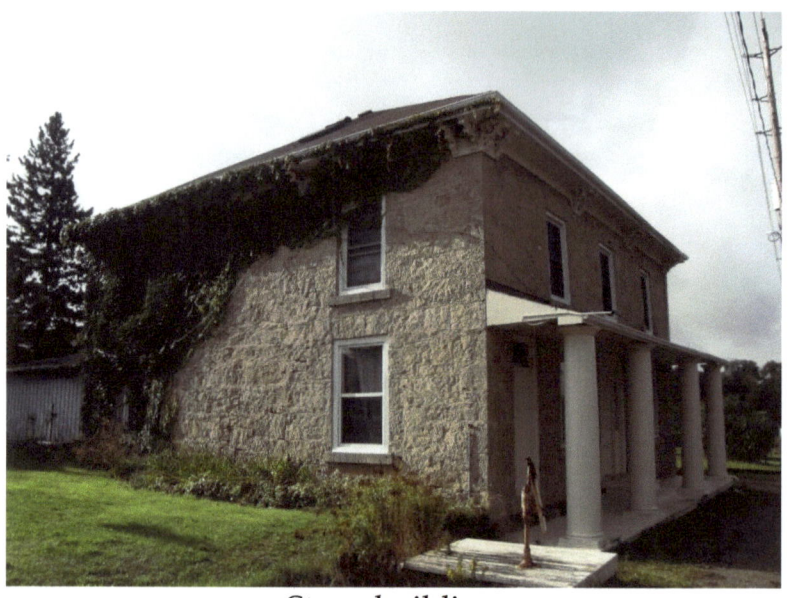

Stone building

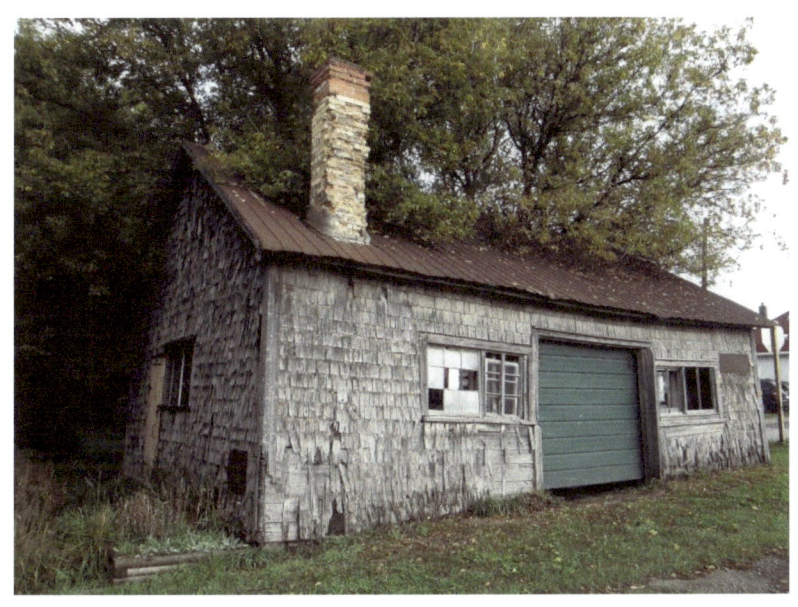

Cedar shakes

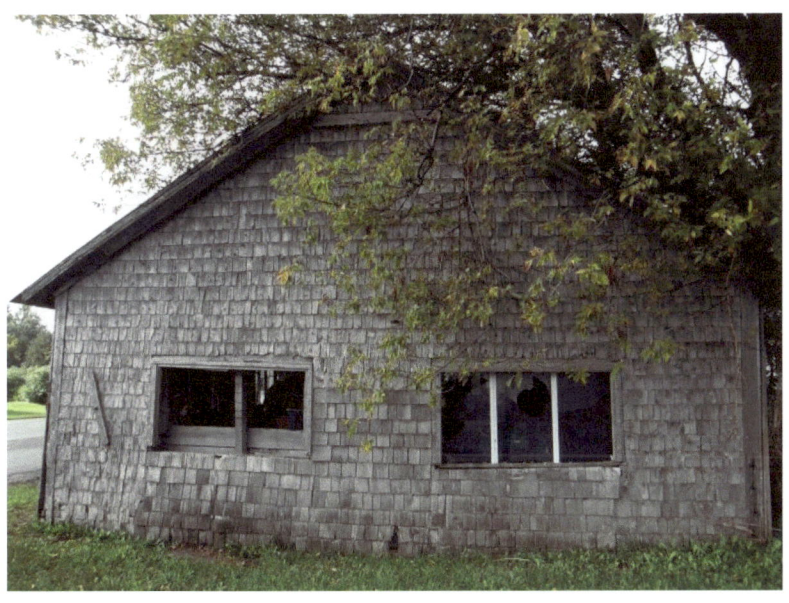

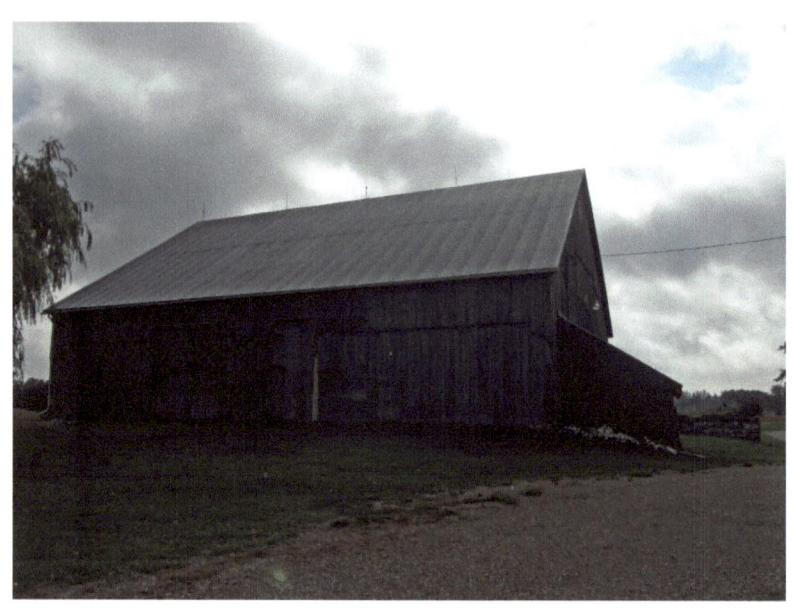

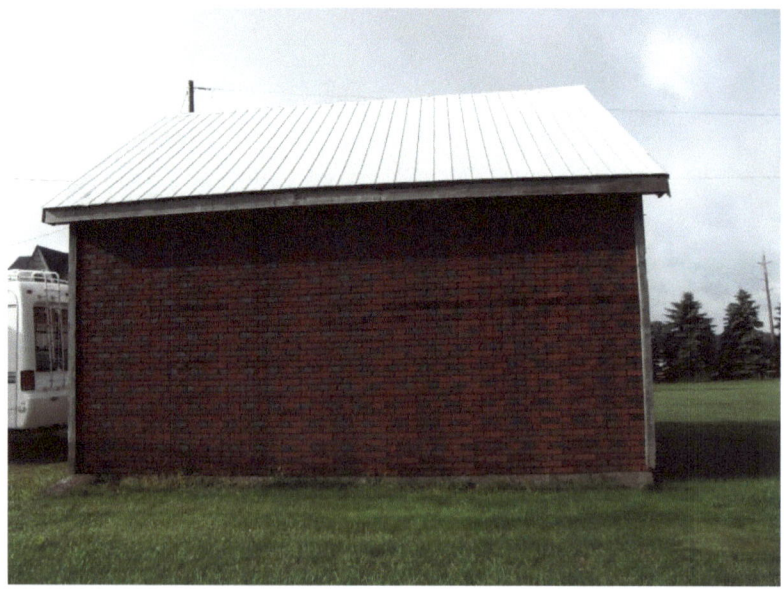

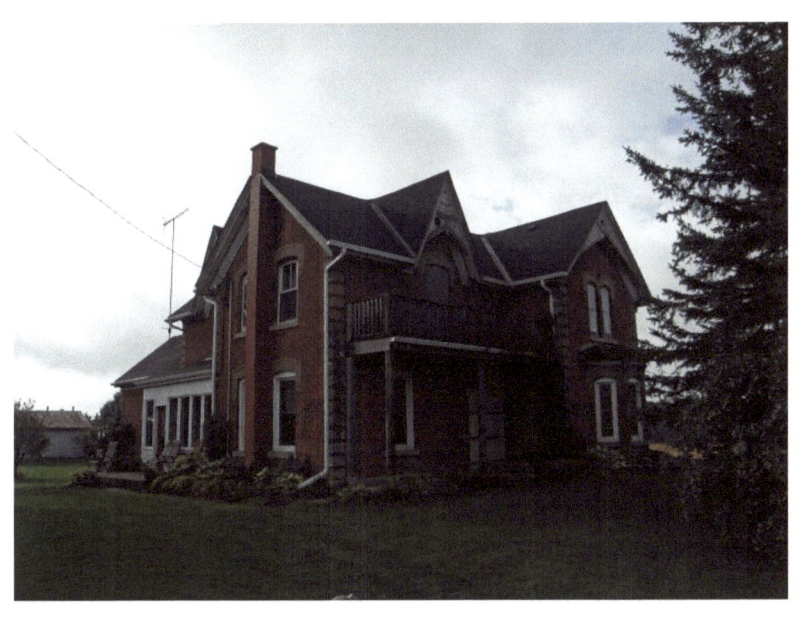

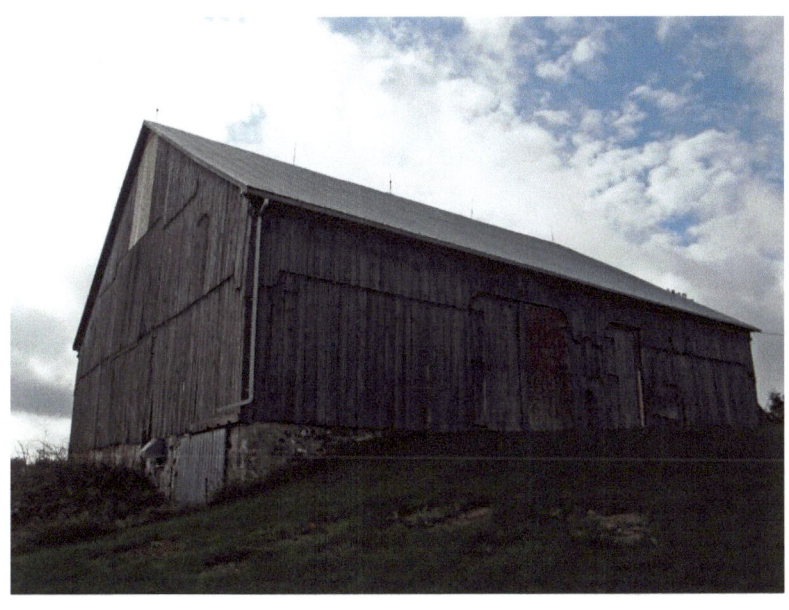

Hillsburgh

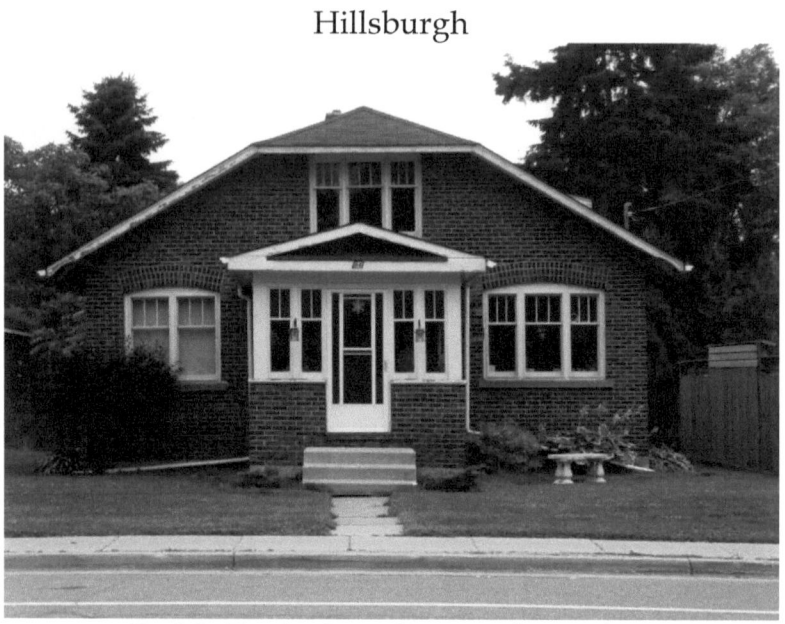

Gothic Revival, pediment above door

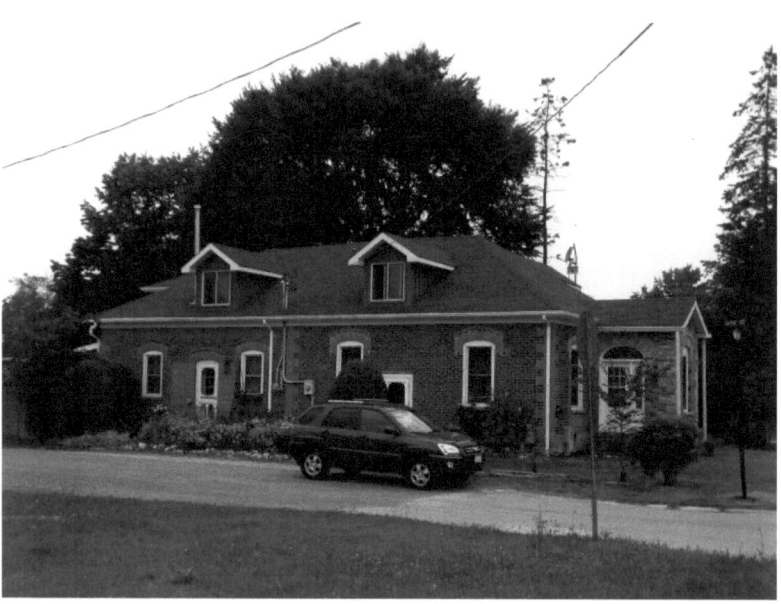

Italianate – corner quoins, arched window voussoirs,
dormers in attic

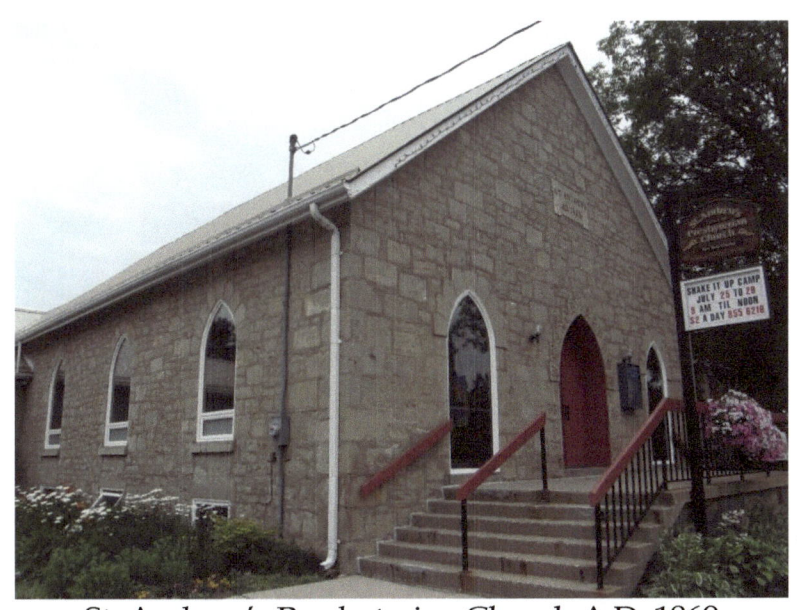

St. Andrew's Presbyterian Church A.D. 1869

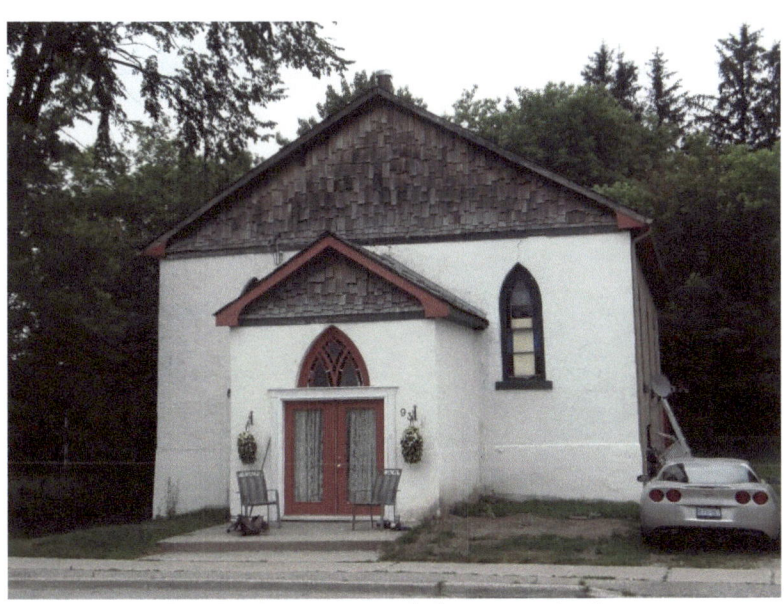

#9 - Gothic Revival, lancet window

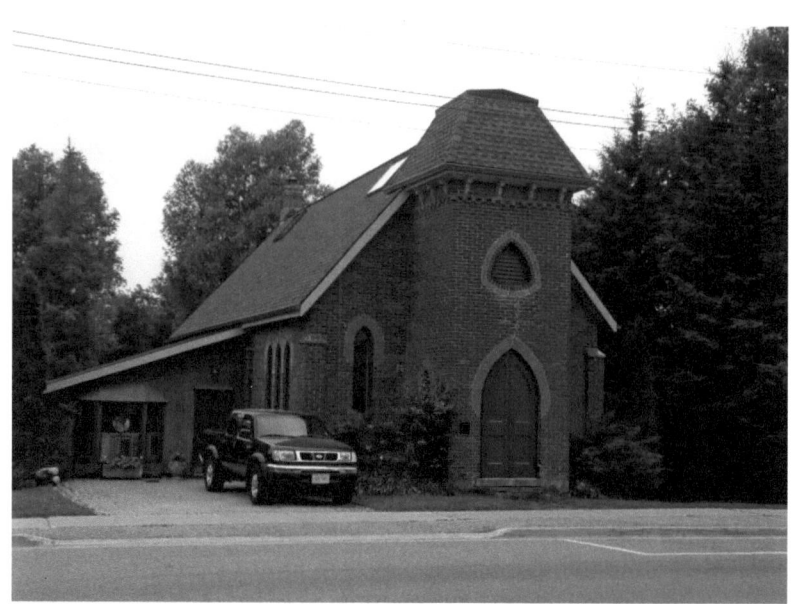

St. John's Anglican Church – 1890s – services held here until about 1918; converted to honey extracting plant – during the war years, with sugar rationing, people filled their own containers from the tanks; lancet windows, cornice brackets on tower

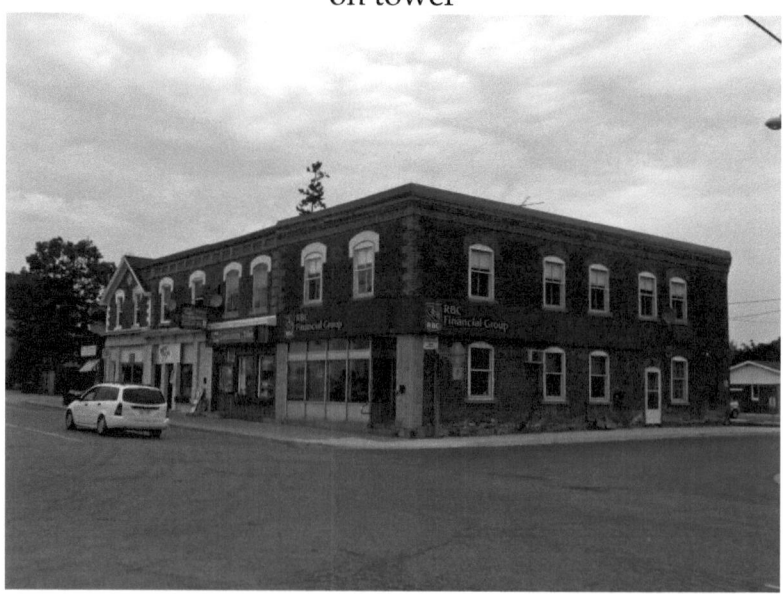

Corner quoins, arched window voussoirs, dentil moulding

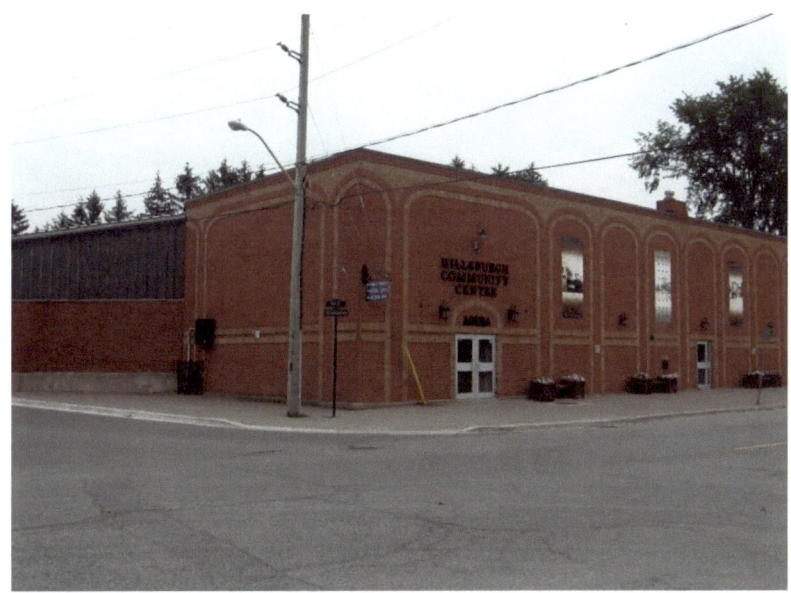

Hillsburgh Community Centre – dichromatic brickwork

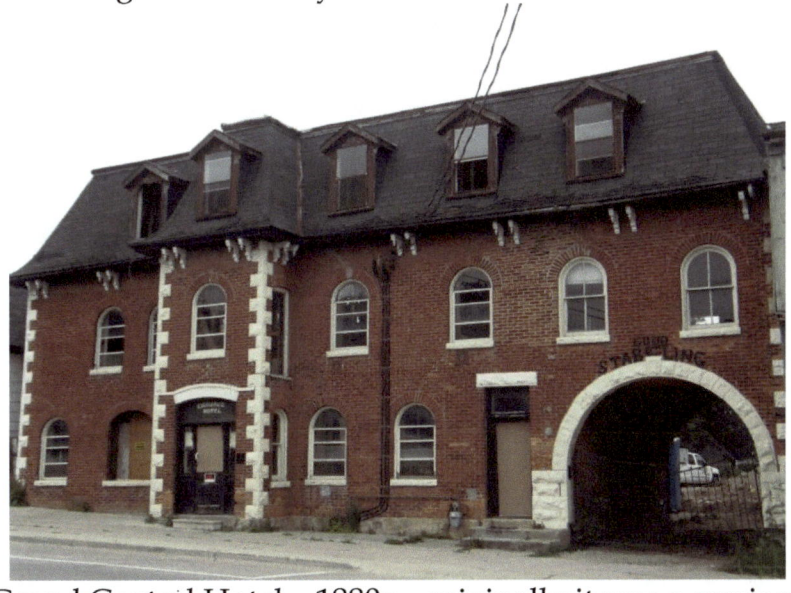

Grand Central Hotel – 1880s – originally it was a carriage works, transformed into a hotel, served as a bank since the early 1900s - Second Empire – mansard roof with dormers, corner quoins, paired cornice brackets

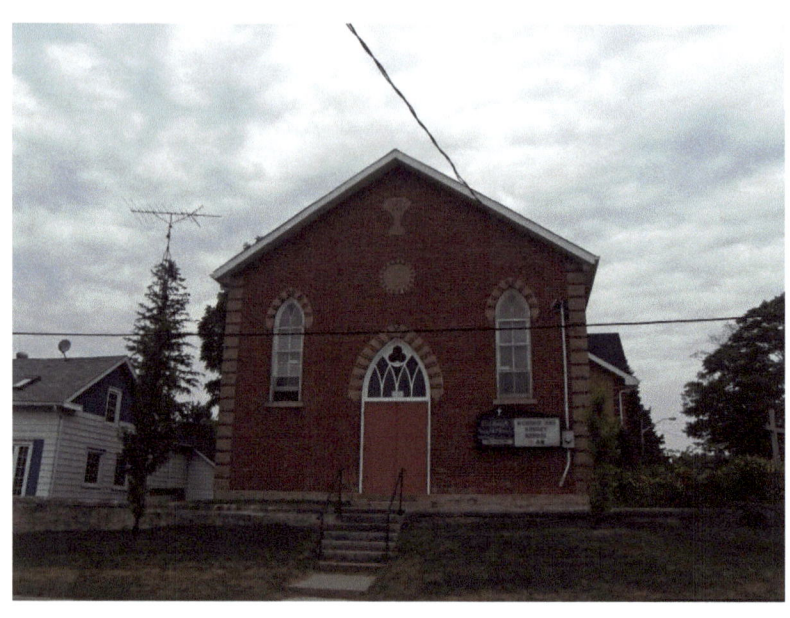

Hillsburgh Baptist Church - 1888
Corner quoins, dichromatic brickwork, lancet windows

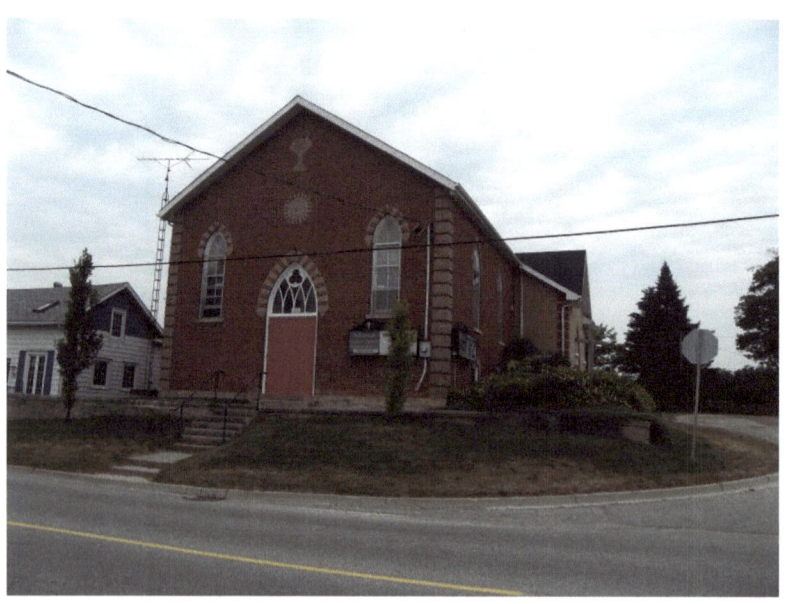

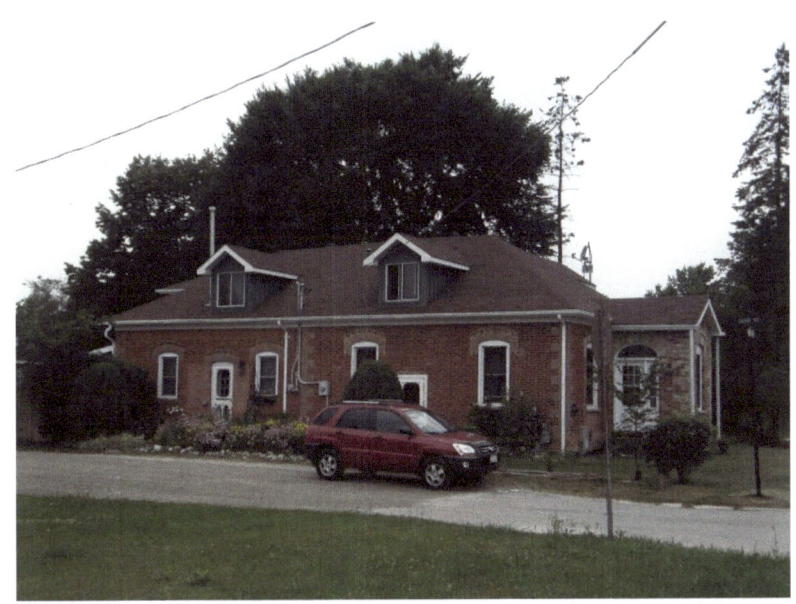

Dichromatic brickwork, corner quoins, dormers, hip roof

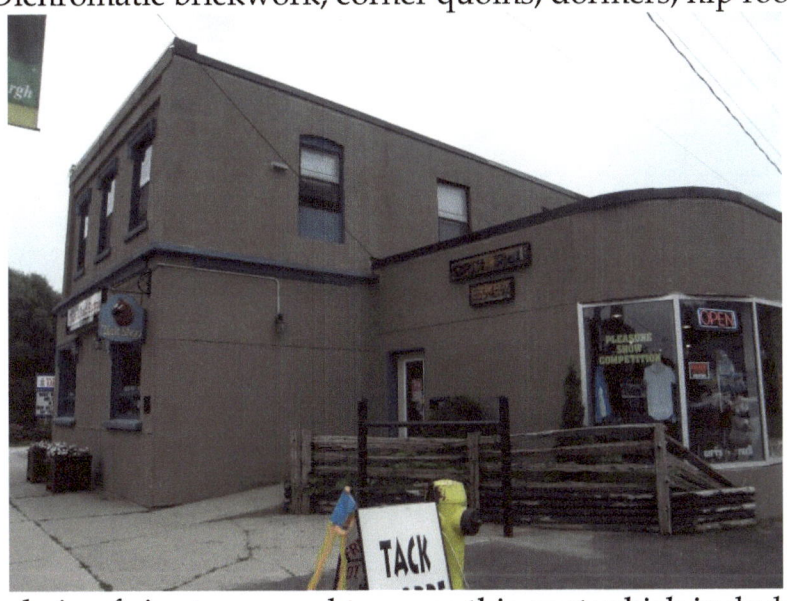

A chain of six stores used to grace this spot which included general stores, Dr. Gibson's drugstore, and butcher shops. The building is most famous for being Canada's first indoor and oldest Chevrolet dealership.

Architectural Terms

Brackets: a decorative or weight-bearing structural element which forms a right angle with one side against a wall and the other under a projecting surface such as an eave or roof. Example: Hillsburgh	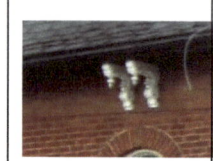
Cobblestone architecture: Refers to the use of cobblestones embedded in mortar as a method for erecting walls on houses and commercial buildings. Example: Eramosa	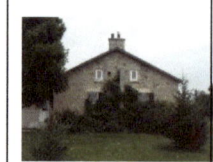
Cornice: originally the wooden overhang of the roof. With the use of stone, brick, iron and steel, the cornice is any projecting shelf at the top of a ceiling or roof. They can be very decorative. Example: Everton	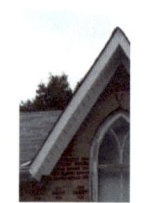
Dichromatic brickwork: the use of two colours of brick, tile or slate to decorate a façade. Example: Hillsburgh	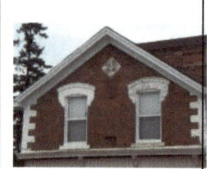
Dormer: (French for "sleep") a gable end window that pierces through the plane of a sloping roof surface to create usable space in the top floor or attic of a building by adding headroom. Example: Hillsburgh	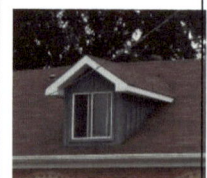

Gable: the triangular portion of a wall between the edges of a sloping roof. Example: Everton	
Hipped Roof: a roof where all sides slope downwards to the walls with no gables. Example: Eden Mills	
Lancet Window: a tall, narrow window with a pointed arch at its top. Example: St. Andrew's Presbyterian Church, Hillsburgh	
Mansard Roof: This style was popularized by Francois Mansart (1598-1666), an accomplished architect of the French Baroque period and especially fashionable during the Second French Empire (1852-1870). This roof is almost flat on the top section, with two slopes on each of its sides with the lower slope at a steeper angle than the upper and having dormer windows. Example: Hillsburgh	

Quoin: masonry blocks at the corner of a wall, often a decorative feature, usually larger or of a different colour than the rest of the wall. Example: Eramosa	
Vergeboards: also called bargeboards – hang from the projecting end of a roof and are often elaborately carved and ornamented. Example: Eramosa	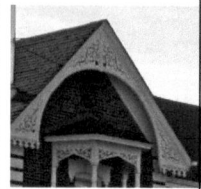

Eden Mills, Eramosa, Everton
and Hillsburgh's Building Styles

Art Moderne, 1930-1945 – This style originated in the United States with rounded corners, smooth walls, and flat roofs. Large expanses of glass were used, even wrapping around corners. Example: Hillsburgh	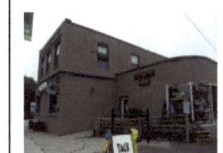
Gothic Revival, 1830-1890 – These decorative buildings have sharply-pitched gables with highly detailed vergeboards, pointed-arch window openings, and dichromatic brickwork. It is a common style in Ontario. Example: Eden Mills Presbyterian Church	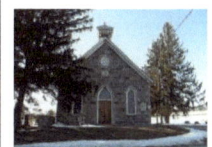
Italianate, 1850-1900 – It has wide-bracketed eaves, belvederes, wrap-around verandahs. Example: Eden Mills	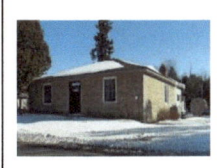

A log cabin, built from logs, was usually one- or 1½-storeys constructed with round rather than hewn, or hand-worked, logs, and erected quickly for frontier shelter. Log cabins were built from logs laid horizontally and interlocked on the ends with notches. The cabin was situated to provide sunlight and drainage so the pioneers could cope better with the rigors of frontier life. The pioneers chose old-growth trees that were straight and had few knots and did not need to be hewn to fit well together. Careful notching minimized the size of the gap between the logs and reduced the amount of chinking with sticks and rocks or daubing with mud to fill the gap. The length of one log was the length of one wall. Several examples in Everton.	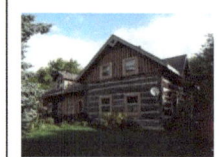
Queen Anne, 1885-1900 – This style is distinguished by an irregular outline featuring a combination of an offset tower, broad gables, projecting two-storey bays, verandahs, multi-sloped roofs, and tall, decorative chimneys. A mixture of brick and wood is common. Windows often have one large single-paned bottom sash and small panes in the upper sash. Example: Eramosa	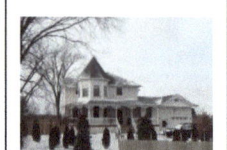
Second Empire, 1860-1880 – The mansard roof is the most noteworthy feature of this style and is evidence of the French origins. Projecting central towers and one or two-storey bays can also be present. Example: Hillsburgh	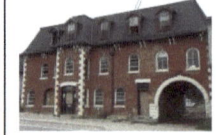